MW01174599

What Makes the World BEAUTIFUL?

By

Pauline Taylor-Bloomfield

Illustrated by: **Roshanay**

What Makes the World Beautiful?
By: Pauline Taylor-Bloomfield

Copyright 2024 Pauline Taylor-Bloomfield.
All rights reserved. No part of this publication may be reproduced, distributed, or transmitted in any form or by any means, including photocopying, recording, or other electronic or mechanical methods, or any information storage and retrieval system, without the prior written permission of the author or publisher, except for brief quotations embodied in critical reviews and certain other commercial uses permitted by copyright law.

For permission requests, contact the publisher at info@ILikeBeingMeBooks.com.
PAPERBACK ISBN: 978-1-998247-03-5
HARDCOVER ISBN: 978-1-998247-02-8
Illustrated by: Roshanay
Published by Burke's Publishing
Published: September, 2024

Dedication

I dedicate this book to my grandchildren, who are curious about the world around them and usually have a thousand questions for us all.

It is my hope that they, and all children growing up in this era, will see beauty in the people, places, and things around them, more often than not.

Together with them, we must continue to work to make our world more beautiful and treasure the gifts given to us by the Creator.

Arinola was a curious girl who always wanted to learn.

She had lots of ideas of her own about the world around her.

At only nine, she was figuring out many things in her world.

Arinola would ask several questions of those in her life, and they would do their best to provide answers to her satisfaction.

Arinola loved the world she was born into and thought it was beautiful.

Arinola saw beauty in spring flowers, floating fall leaves, waves washing up to the shore, colorful butterflies flitting in summer gardens, and the rainbow arch that sometimes appeared in the sky.

She often wondered about what made the
great big world around her so beautiful.

Jumping out of bed on a sunny spring morning, Arinola prepared herself for the day.

All the while, there was one question swirling inside her head.

What makes the world beautiful?

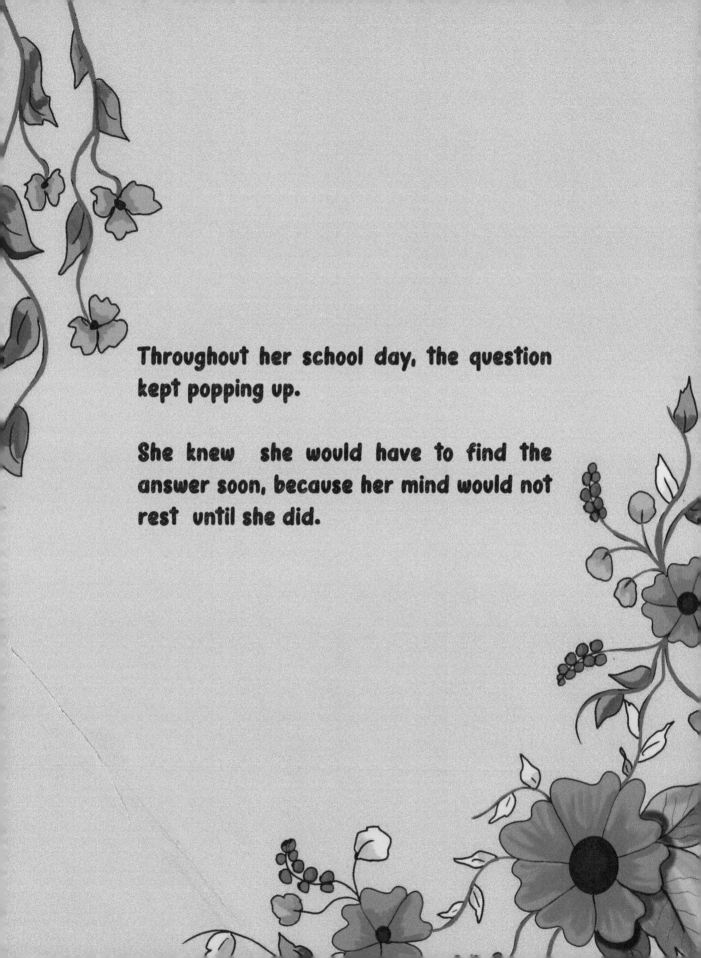

Throughout her school day, the question kept popping up.

She knew she would have to find the answer soon, because her mind would not rest until she did.

Once at home from school, Arinola began her quest for the answer.

Excitedly, she asked her parents,
"What makes the world beautiful?"

Without skipping a beat, they rolled off a long list of things:

- Sunshine to light and warm the earth,

- Colorful leaves dancing in a gust of wind,

- Snow-capped mountain peaks kissing the sky,

- Palm trees bowing as they frame the shore,

- Fragrant fresh smells of nature on an early morning walk,

- Deep blue waters of the seas and oceans,

- Unique animals of all shapes and sizes living on land and in the air and water,

- Delicious harvests from all over the world,

- Taking care of our environment and not wasting our resources.

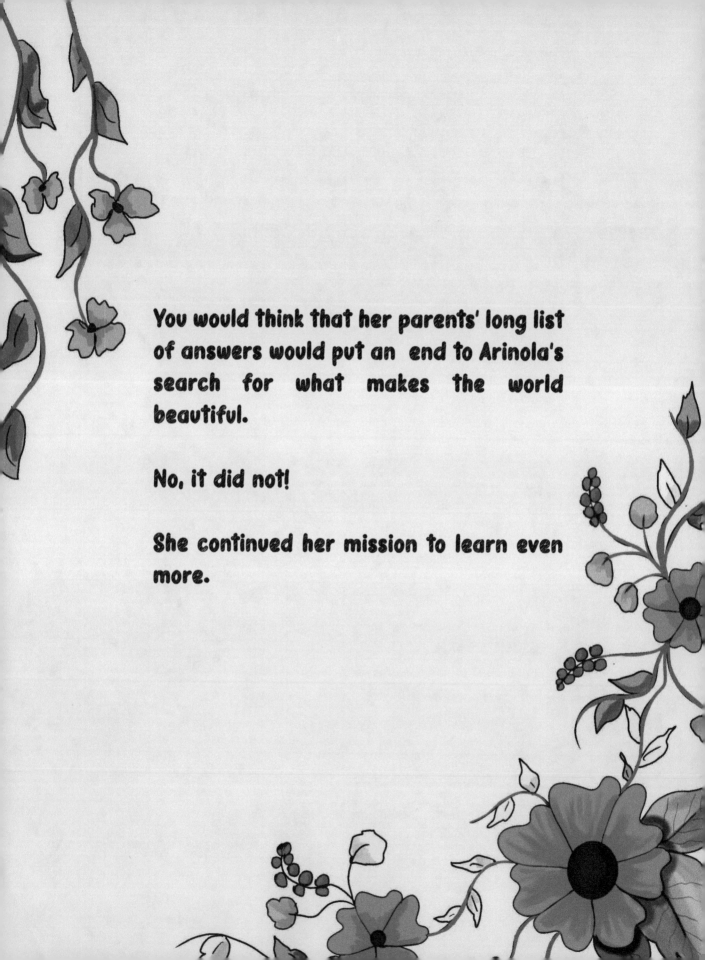

You would think that her parents' long list of answers would put an end to Arinola's search for what makes the world beautiful.

No, it did not!

She continued her mission to learn even more.

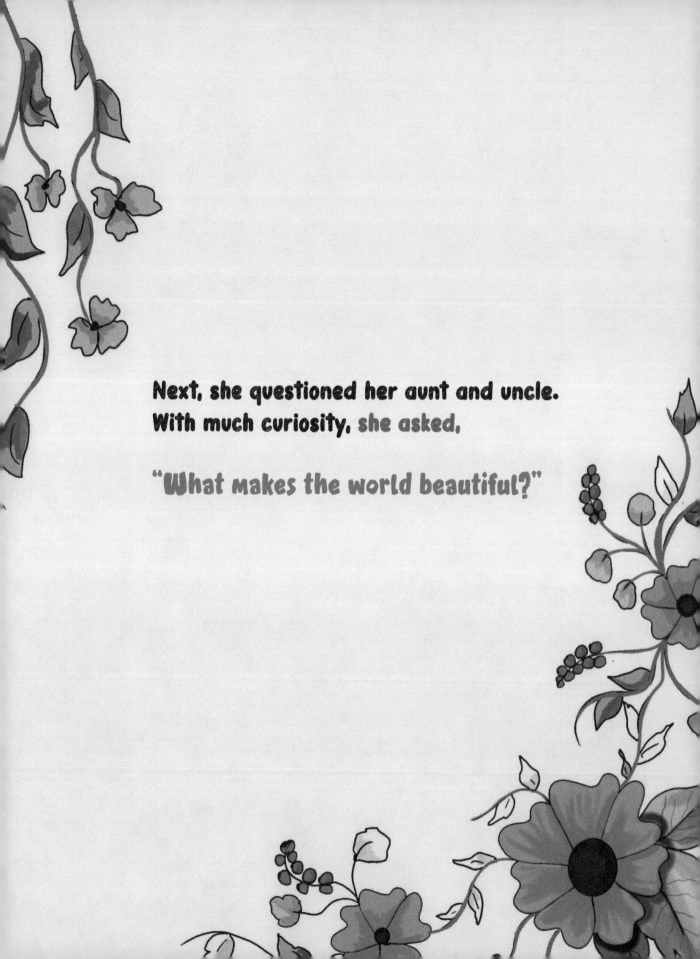

Next, she questioned her aunt and uncle.
With much curiosity, she asked,

"What makes the world beautiful?"

They replied

- Thrilling musical tunes from birds in the air,

- The night sky with its bright moon and trillions of twinkling stars,

- The pitter patter of rainfall that lulls us

- Musical notes struck on instruments of the orchestra, and the sounds of the steel pan and djembe drum,

- Bodies moving rhythmically in time and space, showing their skills through sports and dance,

- People celebrating and honoring different traditions and cultures in harmony.

Hmm, thought Arinola. These are all wonderful reasons, but there must be more to it.

She would continue her search for the answer, although it would have to wait until the next day at school.

The next day, Arinola asked her teacher,

"What makes the world beautiful?"

Her teacher said:

- Hands reaching out to help and share with others,

- Using kind and polite words with each other,

- Freedom to be the best we are meant to be.

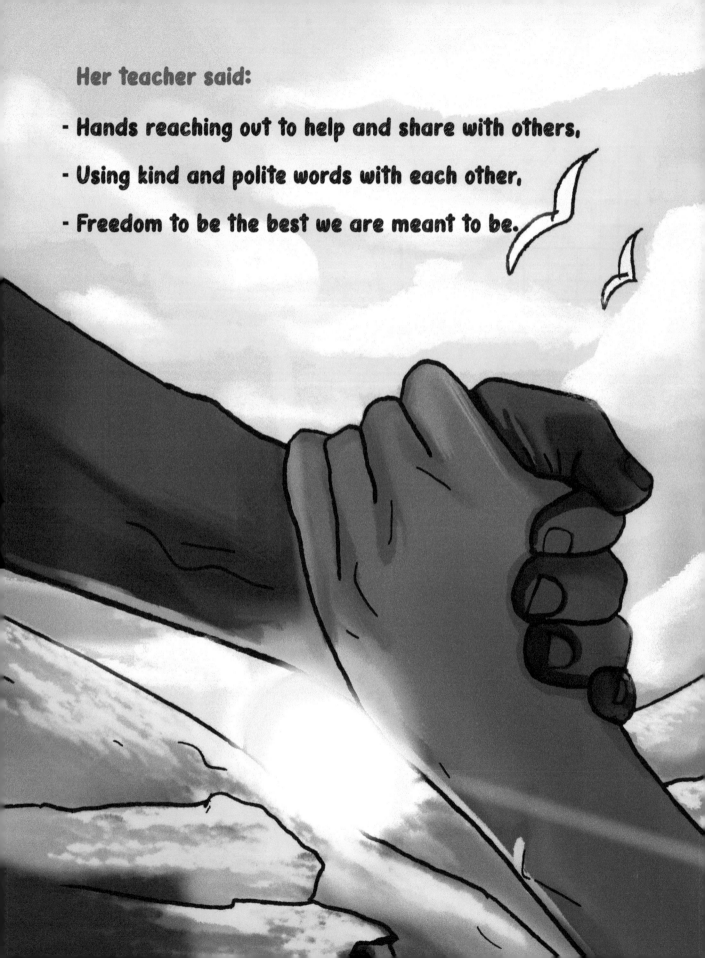

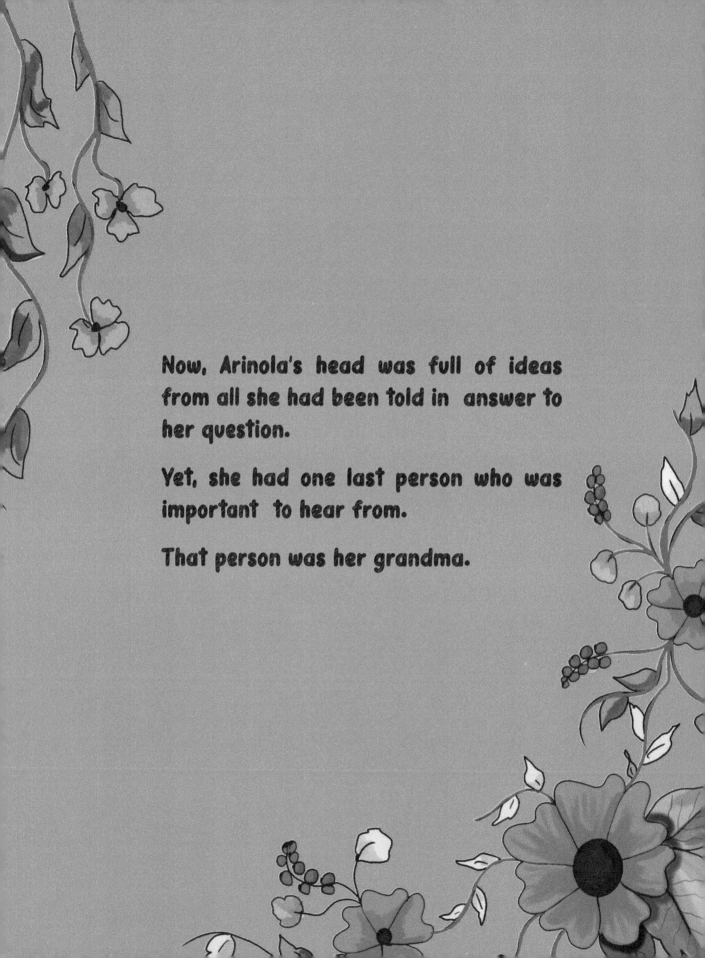

Now, Arinola's head was full of ideas from all she had been told in answer to her question.

Yet, she had one last person who was important to hear from.

That person was her grandma.

So, Arinola called her grandma that evening after dinner.

In a loud and friendly voice, she asked,

"What makes the world beautiful?"

To her great surprise, her grandma's response was, "My beautiful child, don't you mean WHO makes the world beautiful?"

It was at that very moment that images popped into her head.

She saw her dad and mom planting their summer garden; her friends dancing to the beat of joyful music; and her teacher helping her classmates learn and solve problems.

Arinola was beginning to see more clearly the beauty that surrounded her in the world.

Who Am I?

I take care of your teeth.

Who Am I?

I bring the mail to your home.

Who Am I?

I grow your food.

Who Am I?

I take care of you when you are sick.

Who Am I?

**I give you medicine
to make you feel better.**

Who Am I?

I make sure you are safe.

Who Am I?

I build structures for you to live, work and play in.

She thought and thought about all she had heard from her parents, aunt and uncle, and teacher.

She remembered her grandma's wise words as well. All their answers filled her heart and mind. They quelled her curiosity.

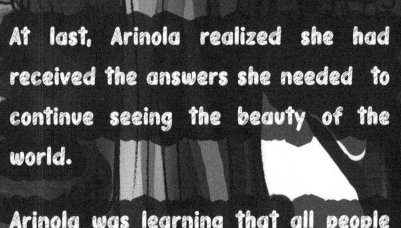

At last, Arinola realized she had received the answers she needed to continue seeing the beauty of the world.

Arinola was learning that all people have a part to play in making our world even more beautiful.

THE END

Reading Activities

1 Arinola's parents made a list of what makes the world beautiful. What do you think makes the world beautiful?

----

2 Who changed Arinola's thinking about her question?

How?_____

3 Arinola surveyed her parents, aunt and uncle, teacher, and grandma during her quest. Why do you think she asked these people?

----

4 Why do you think her grandma said who instead of what?

----

5 Can you think of a time when you used a list?

----

6 Name someone who may need to use a list.

----

7 Where else would you see a list used?

----

8 Was Arinola happy with what she found out? How do you know?

----

9 What did you learn from this story?

----

10 What can you do to keep the world beautiful?

Rate this Book

Lowest ★ ★ ★ ★ ★ Highest
 1   2   3   4   5

What is your rating? ----------------------------------

Why? --

Share your thinking. ------------------------------

www.ingramcontent.com/pod-product-compliance
Lightning Source LLC
Jackson TN
JSHW071210231224
75609JS00001BA/2

* 9 7 8 1 9 9 8 2 4 7 0 2 8 *